unicorn coloring book for kids ages 4 - 8

copyright © 2020 all rights reserved
no part of this publication may be reproduced , distributed , or transmitted
in any form or by any means , including photocopying , recording
without the prior written permission of the publisher .

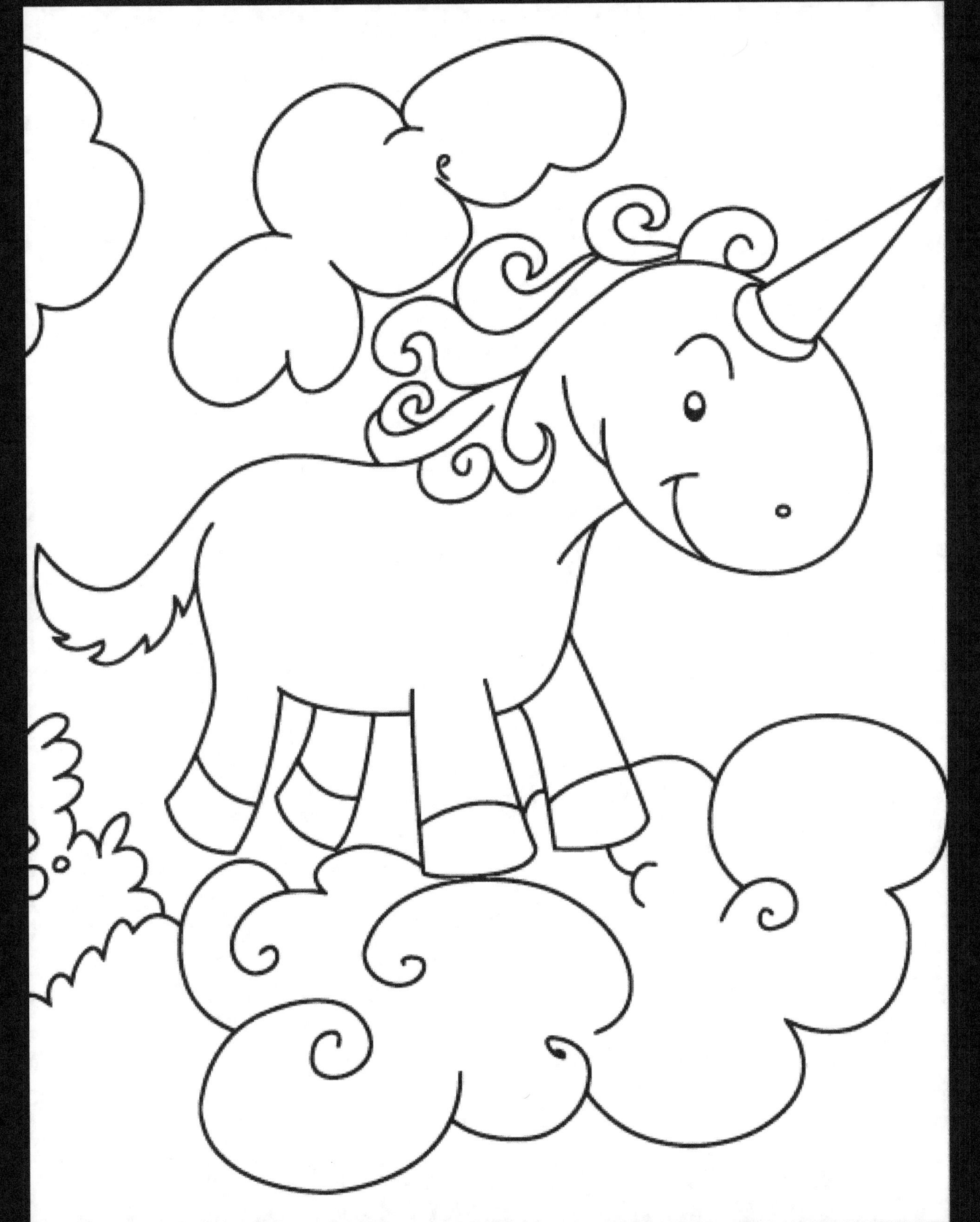

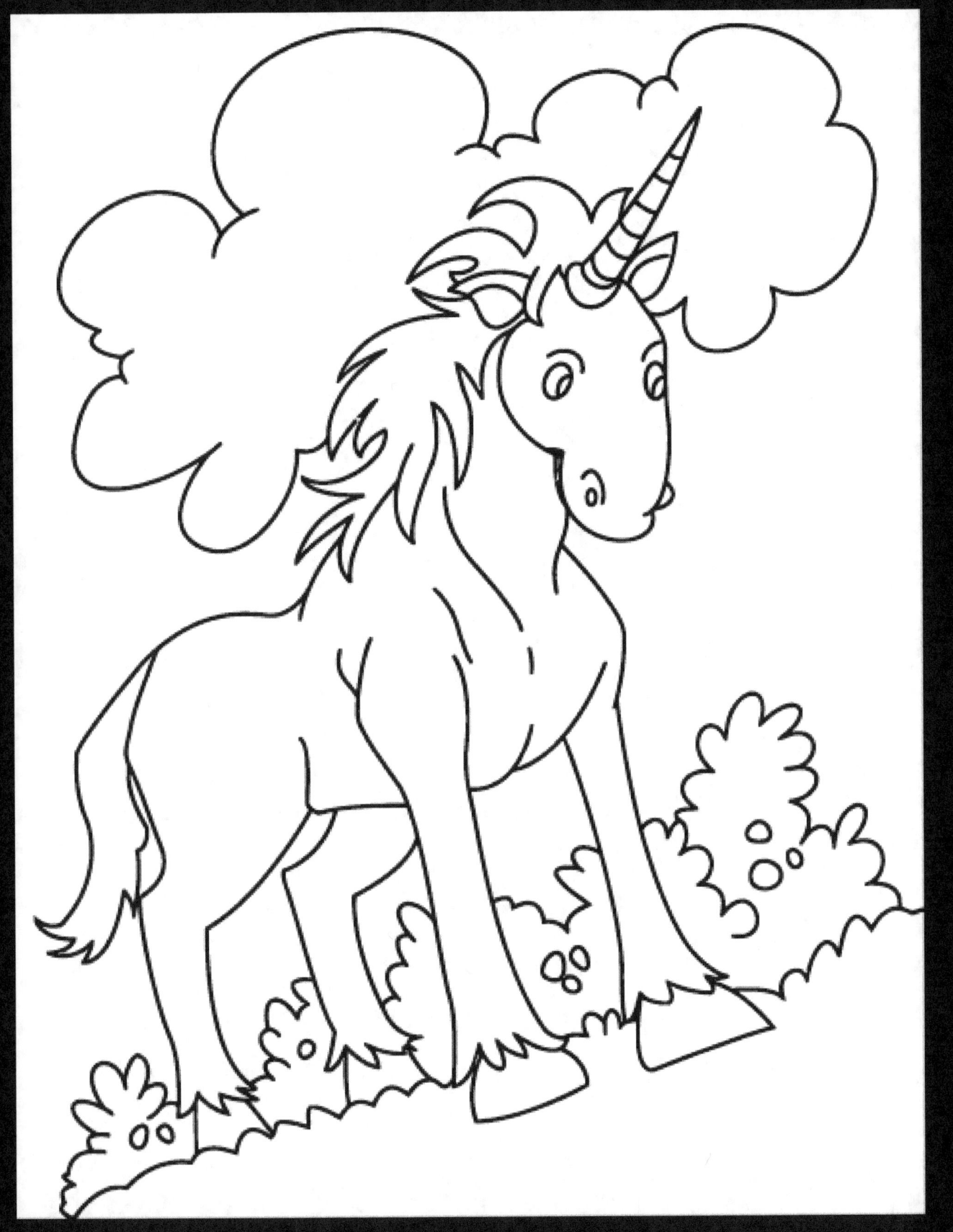

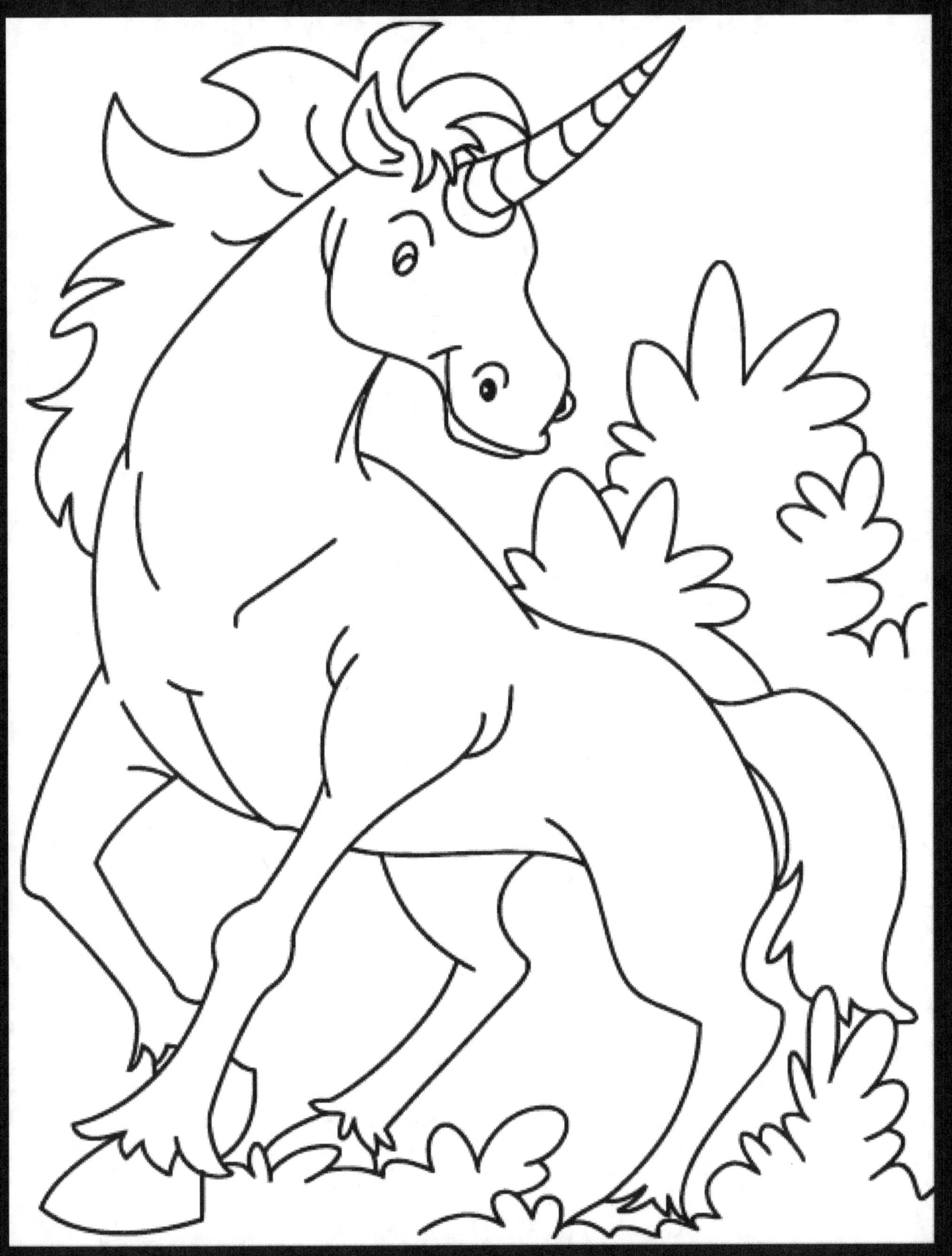

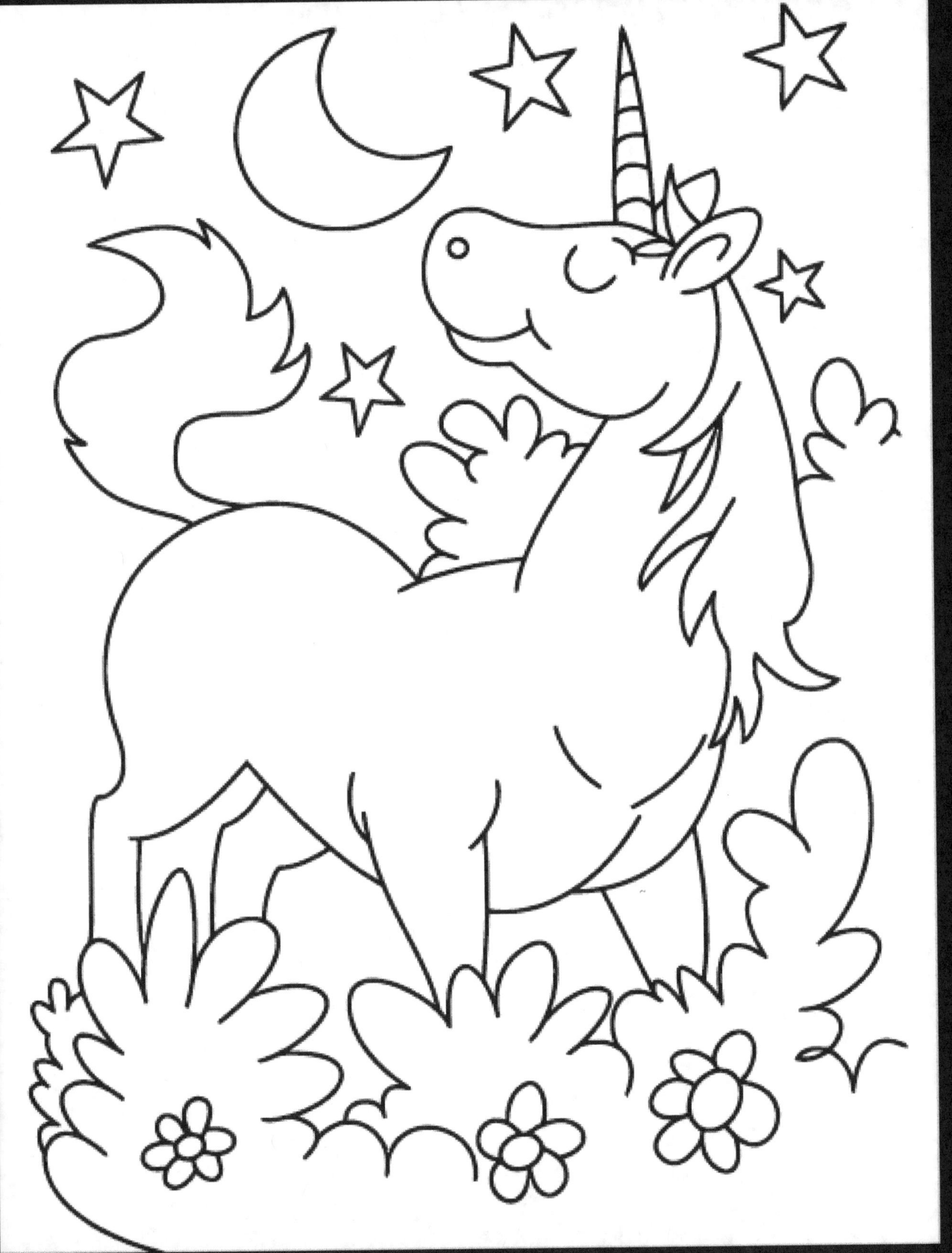

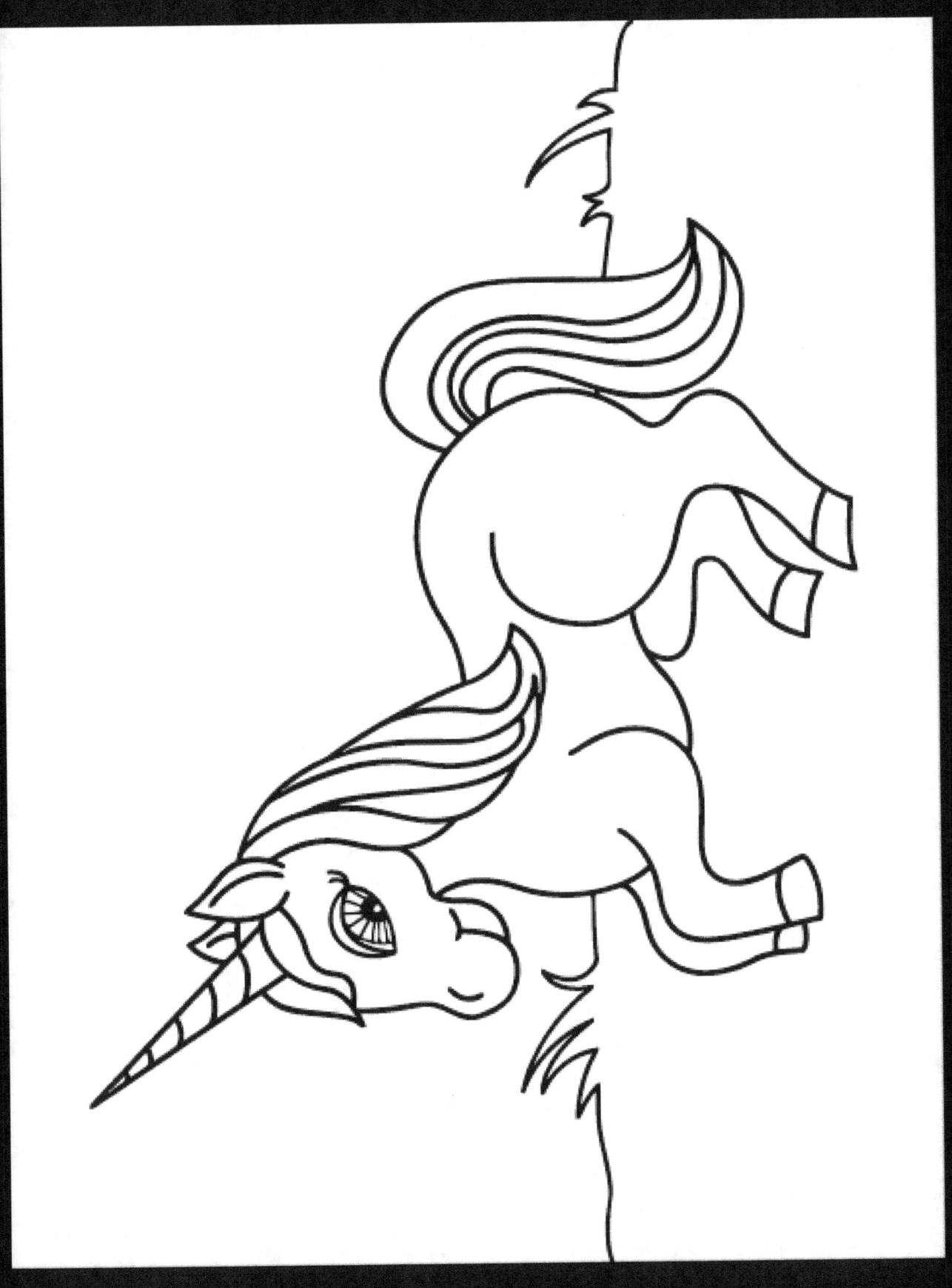

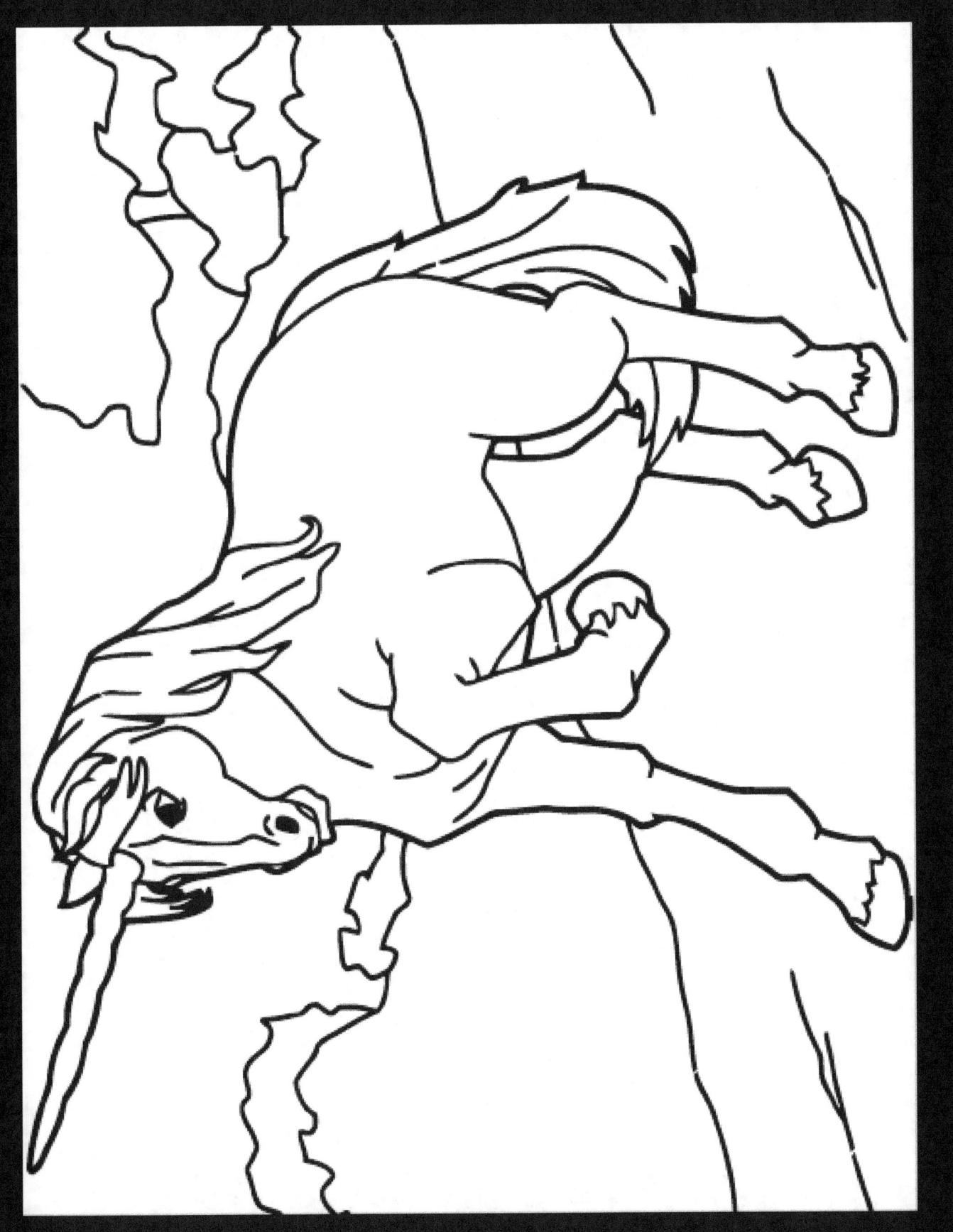

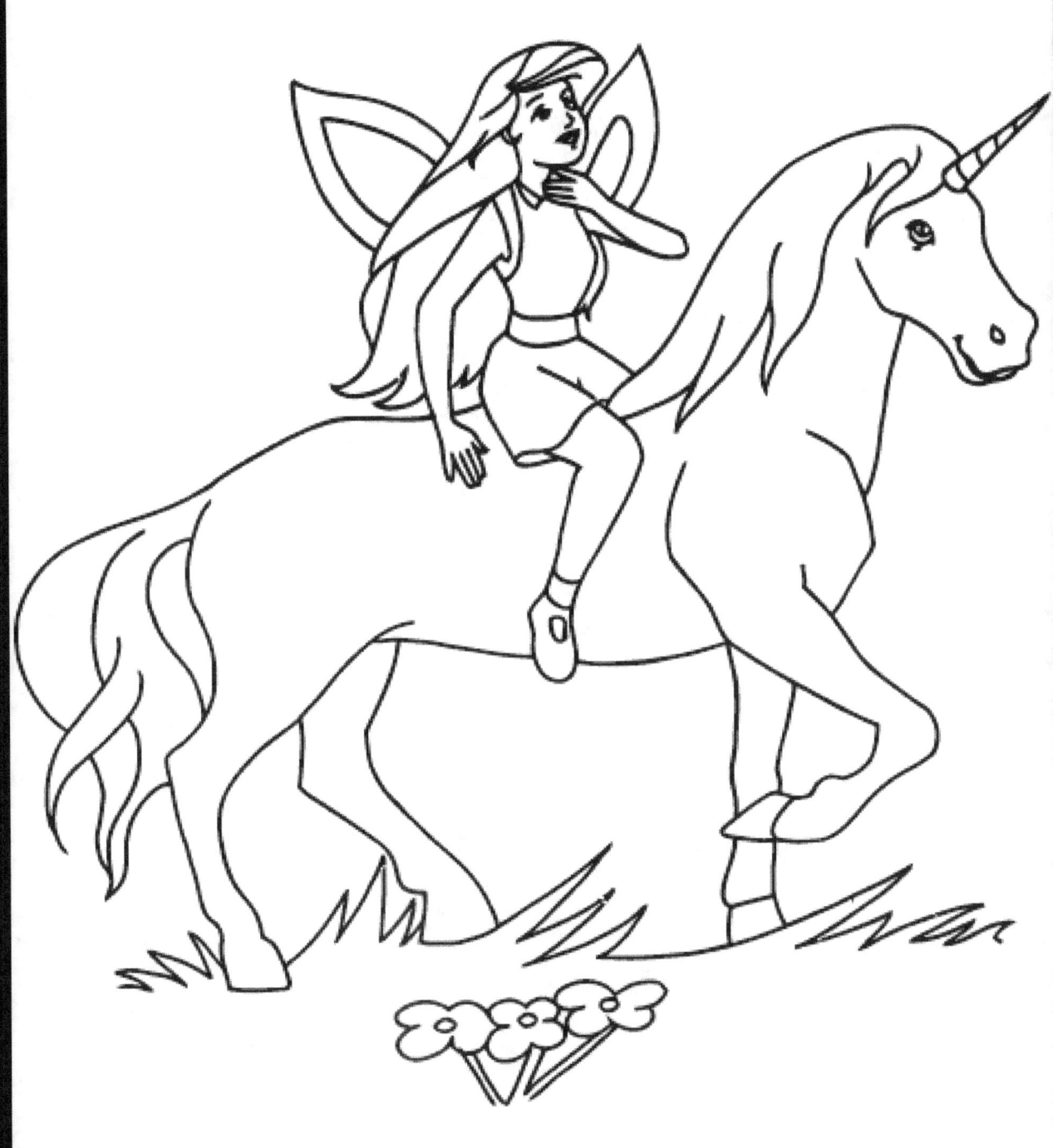

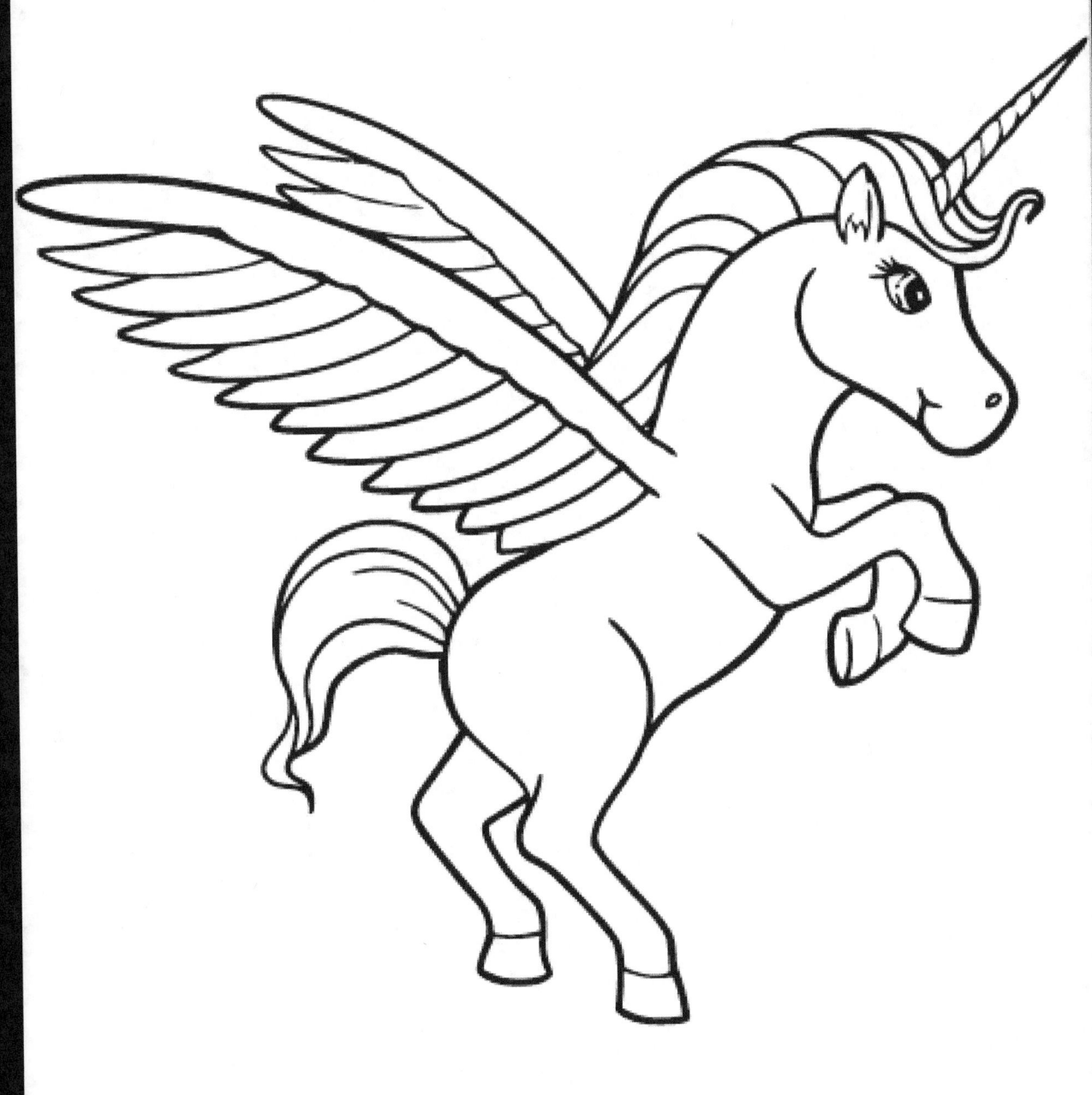

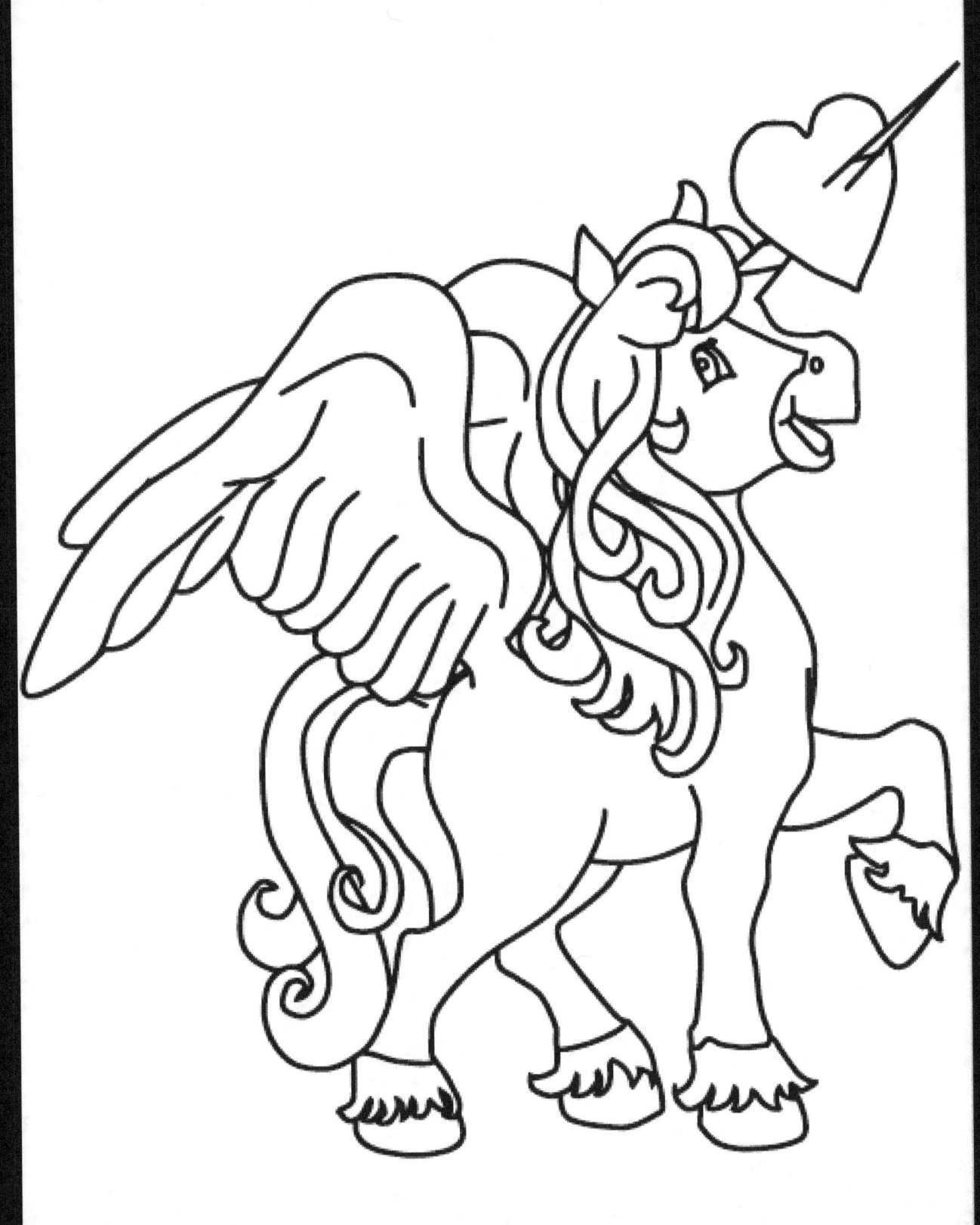

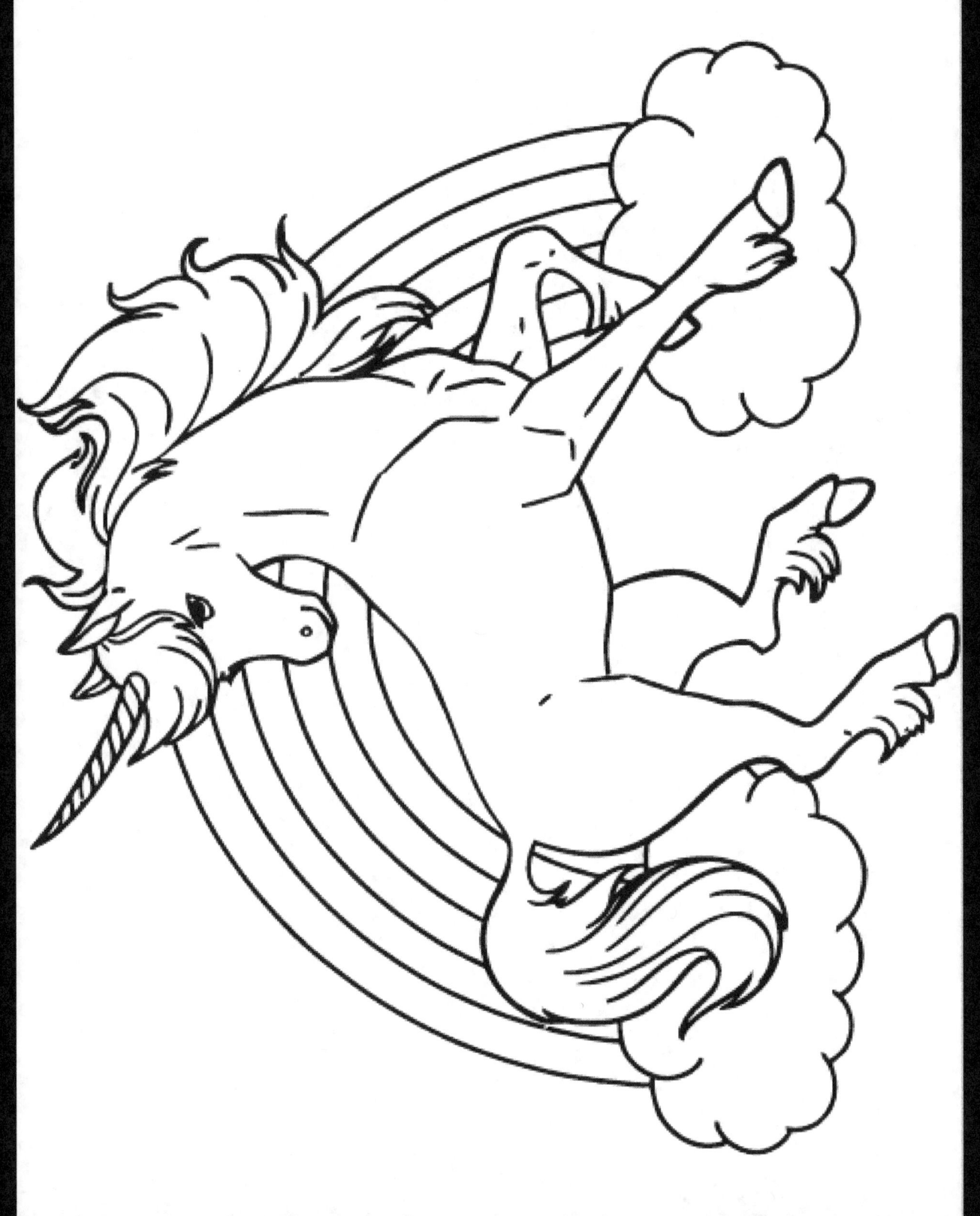

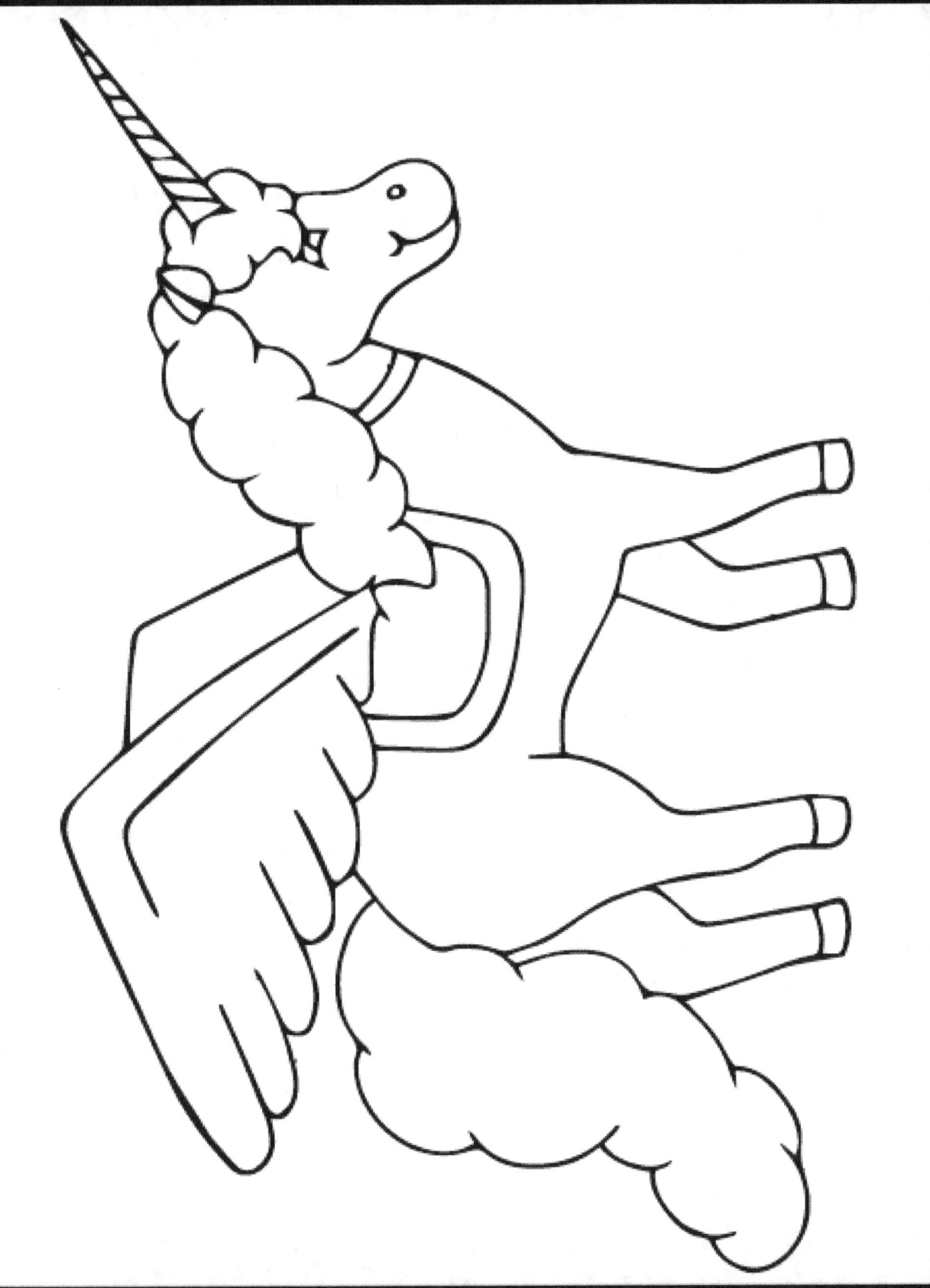

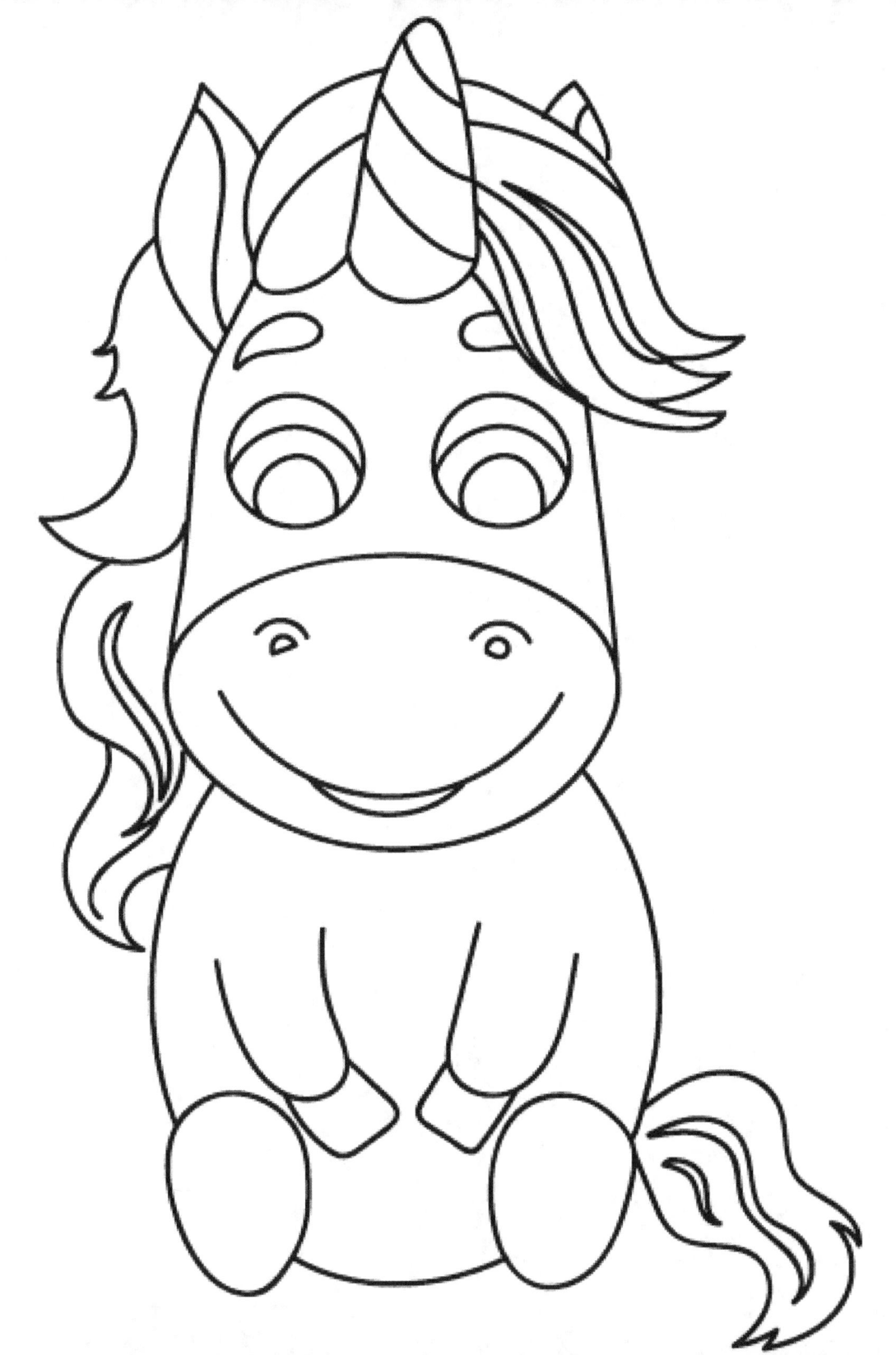

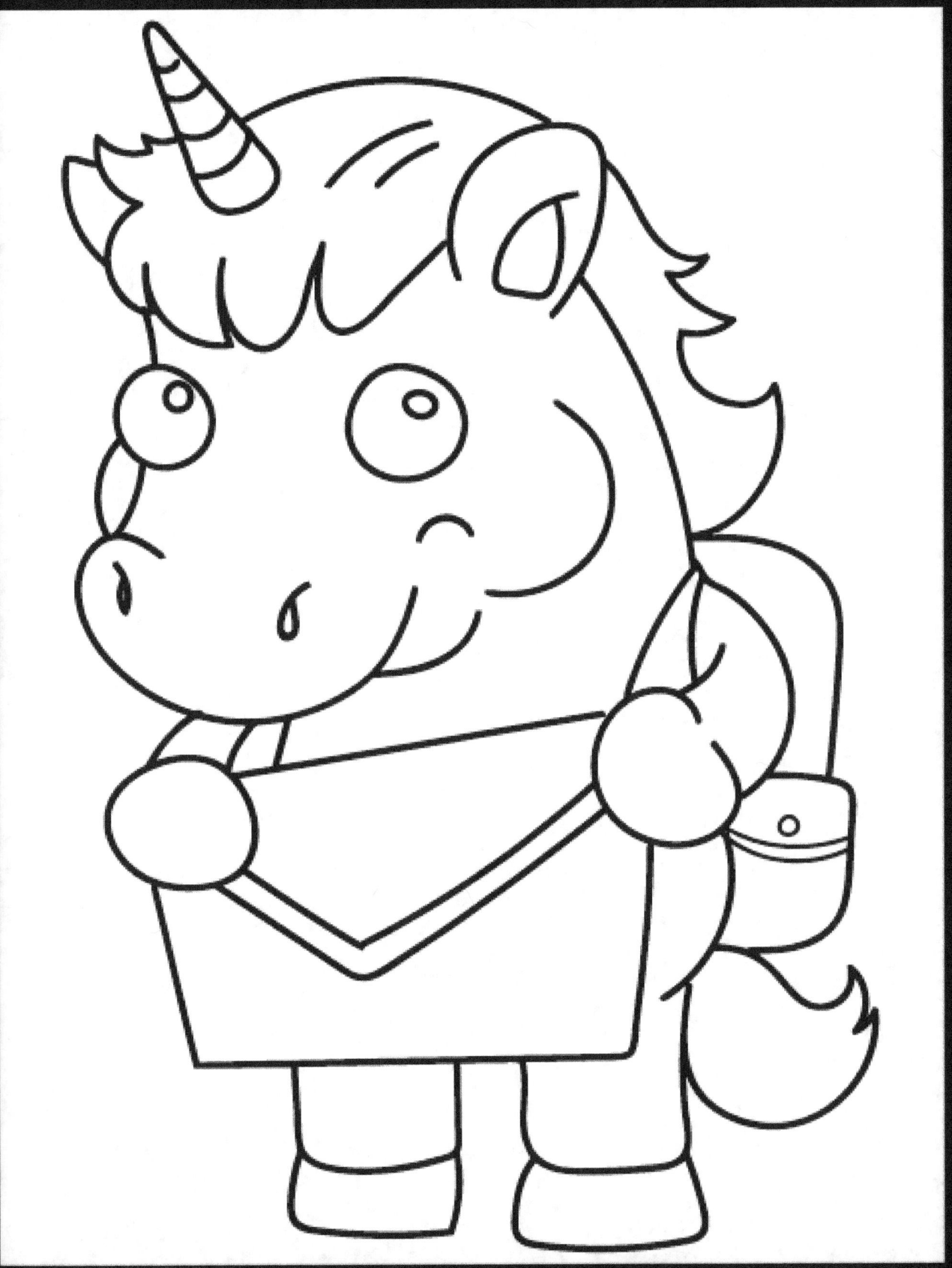

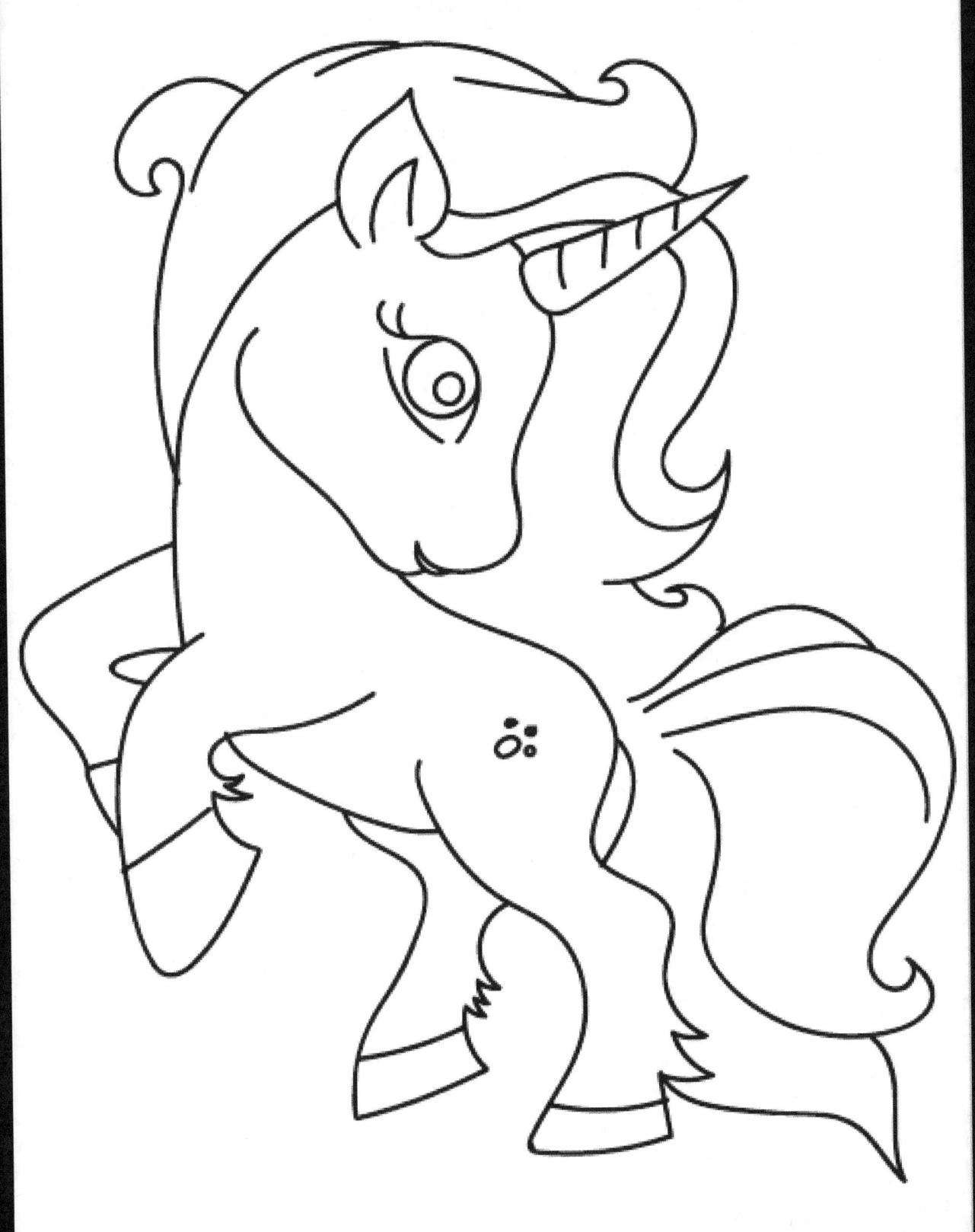

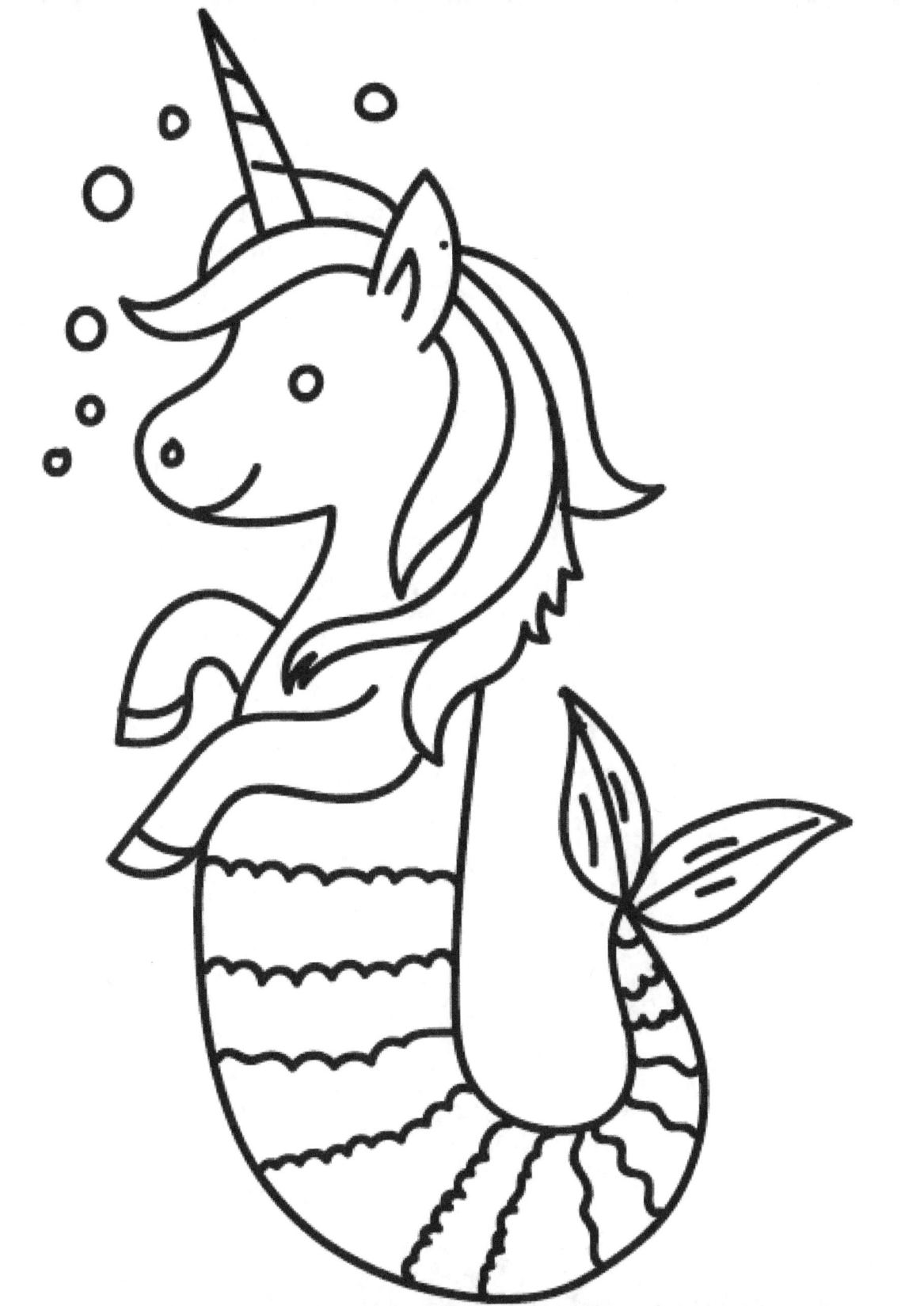

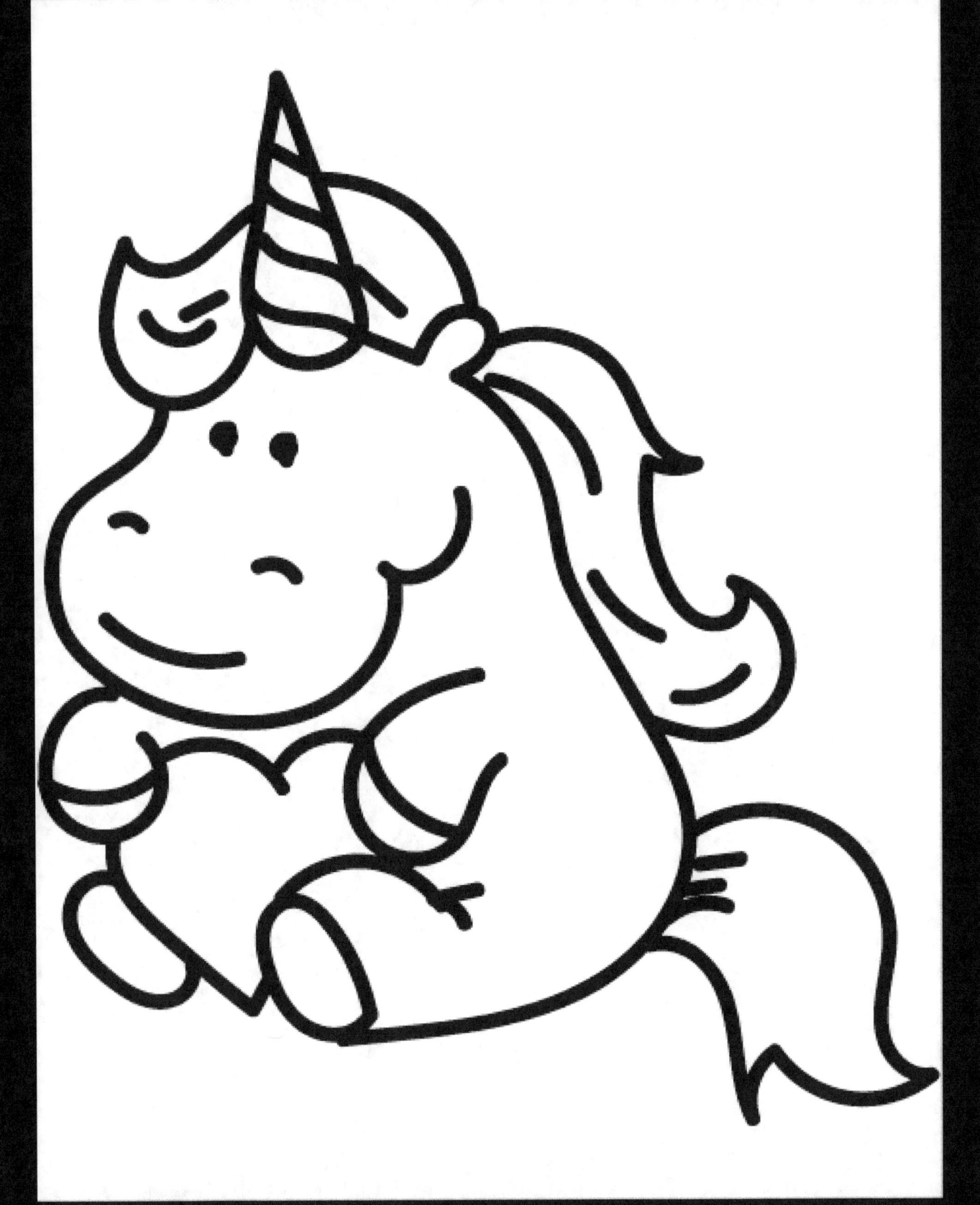

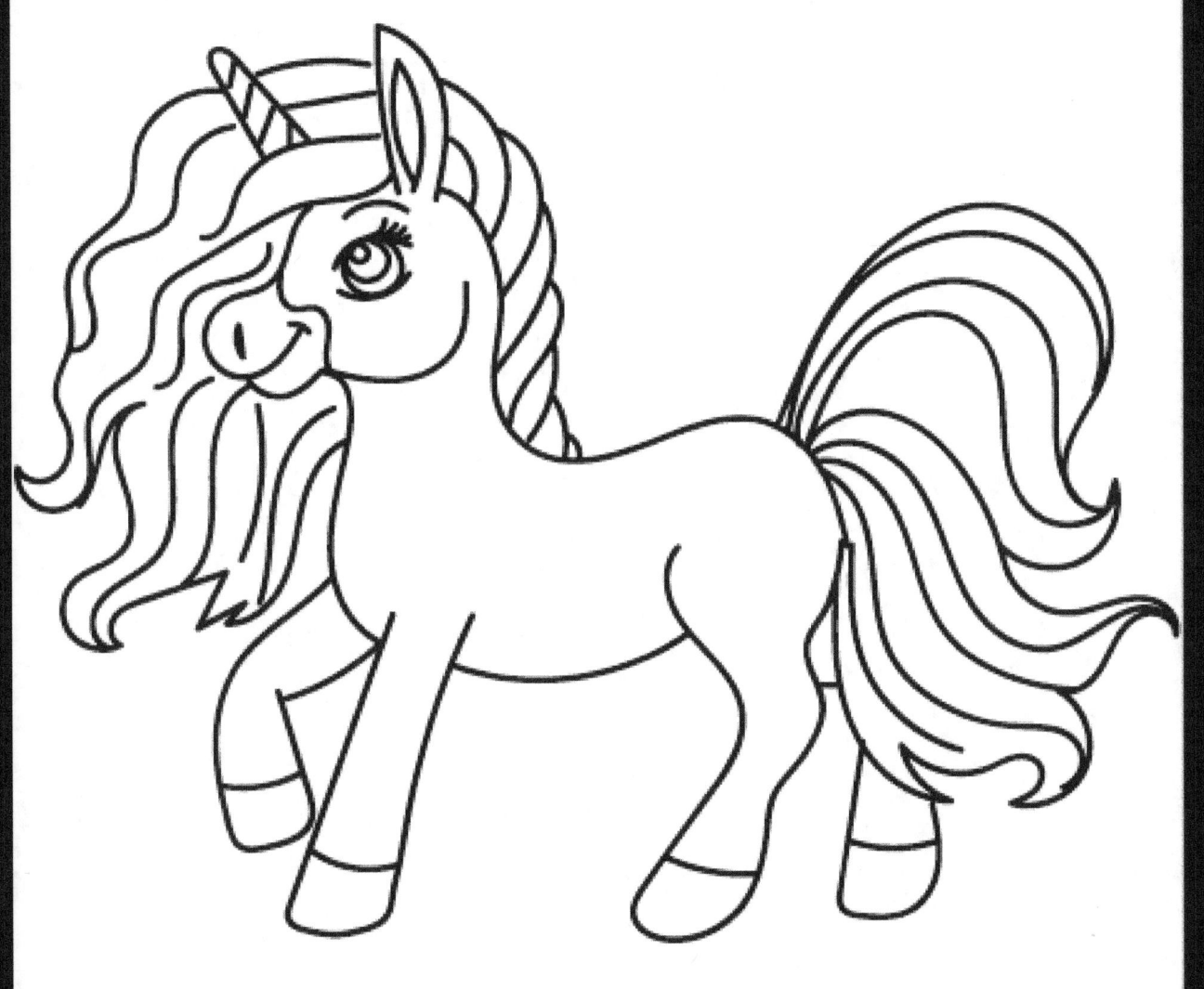

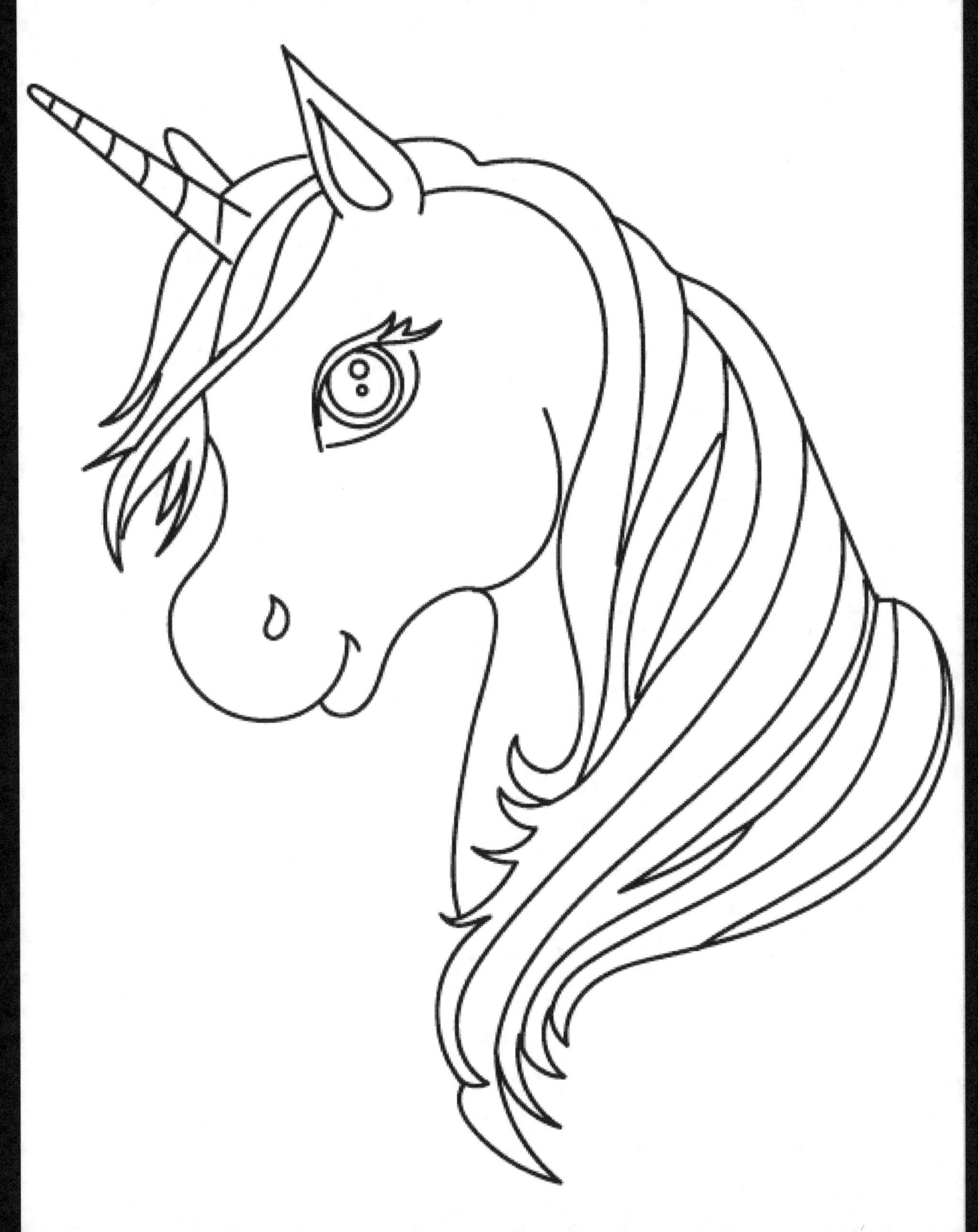

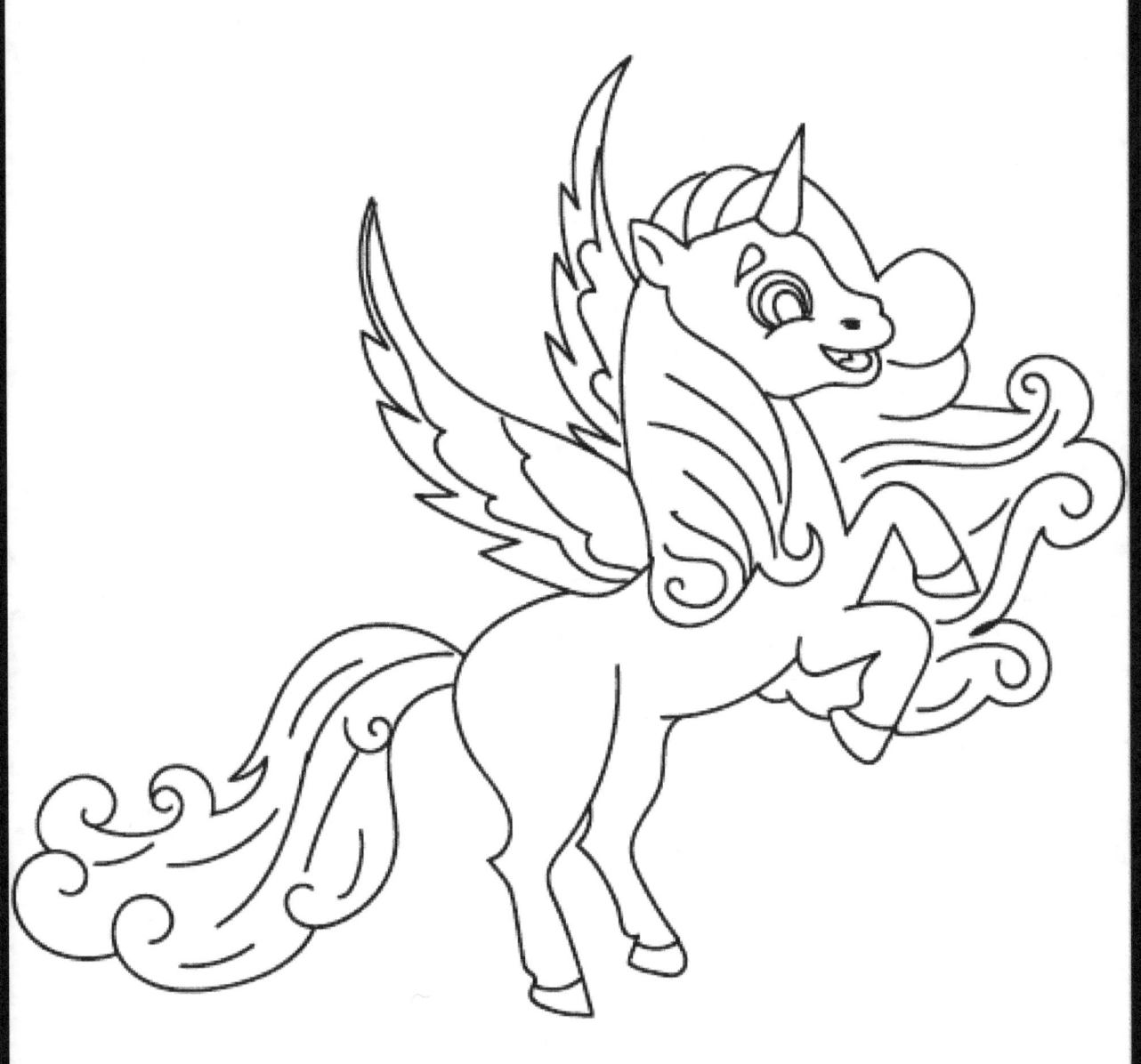

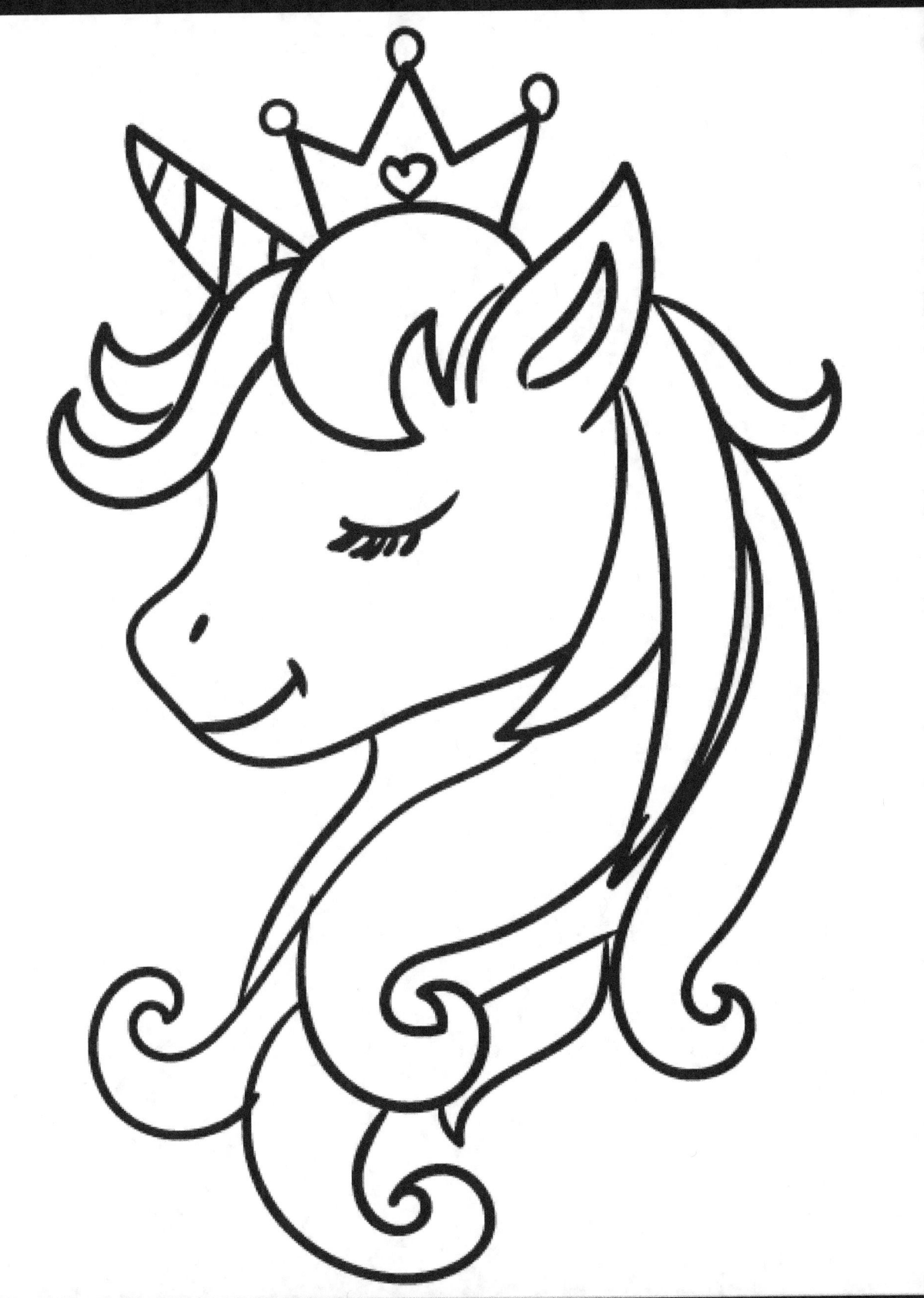

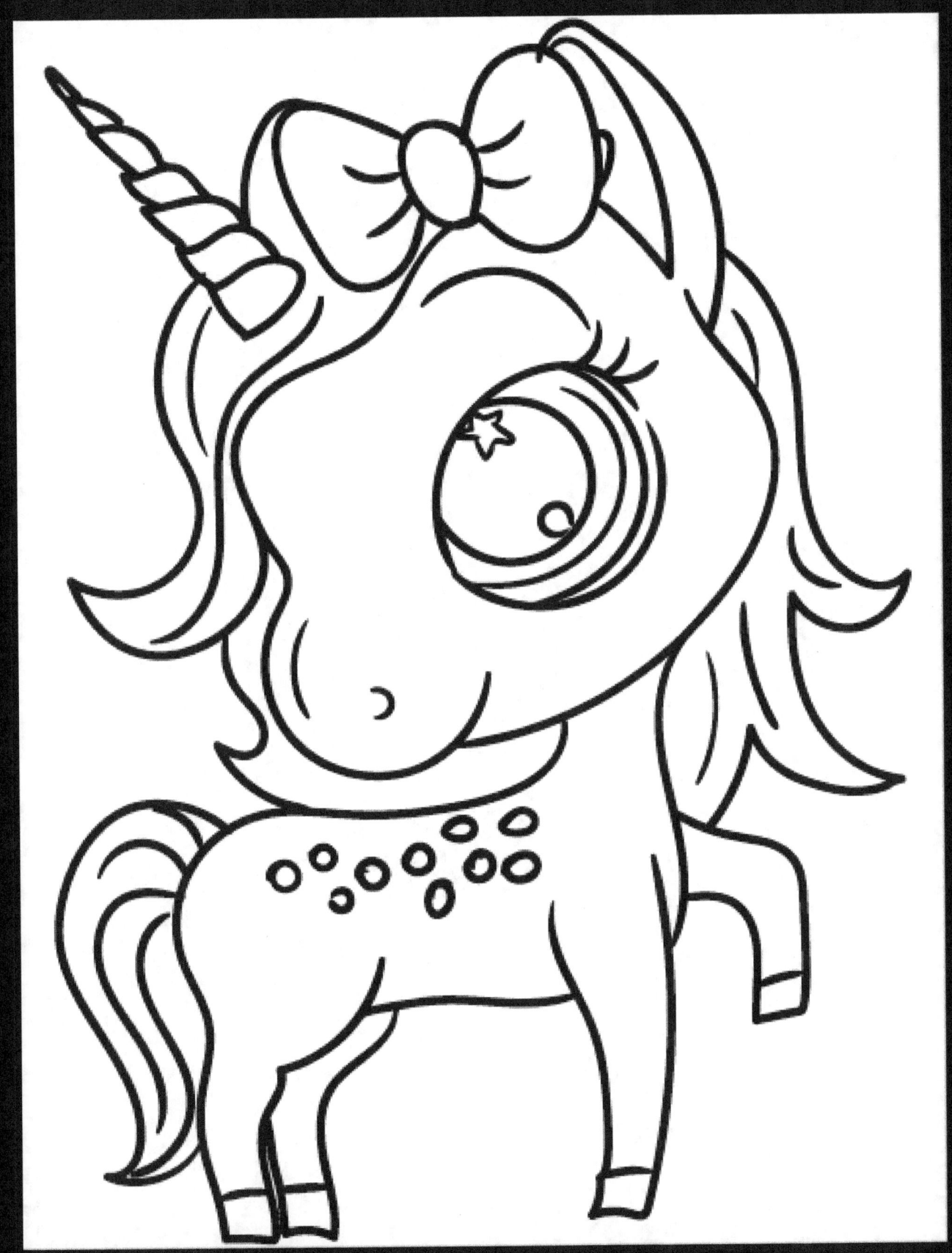

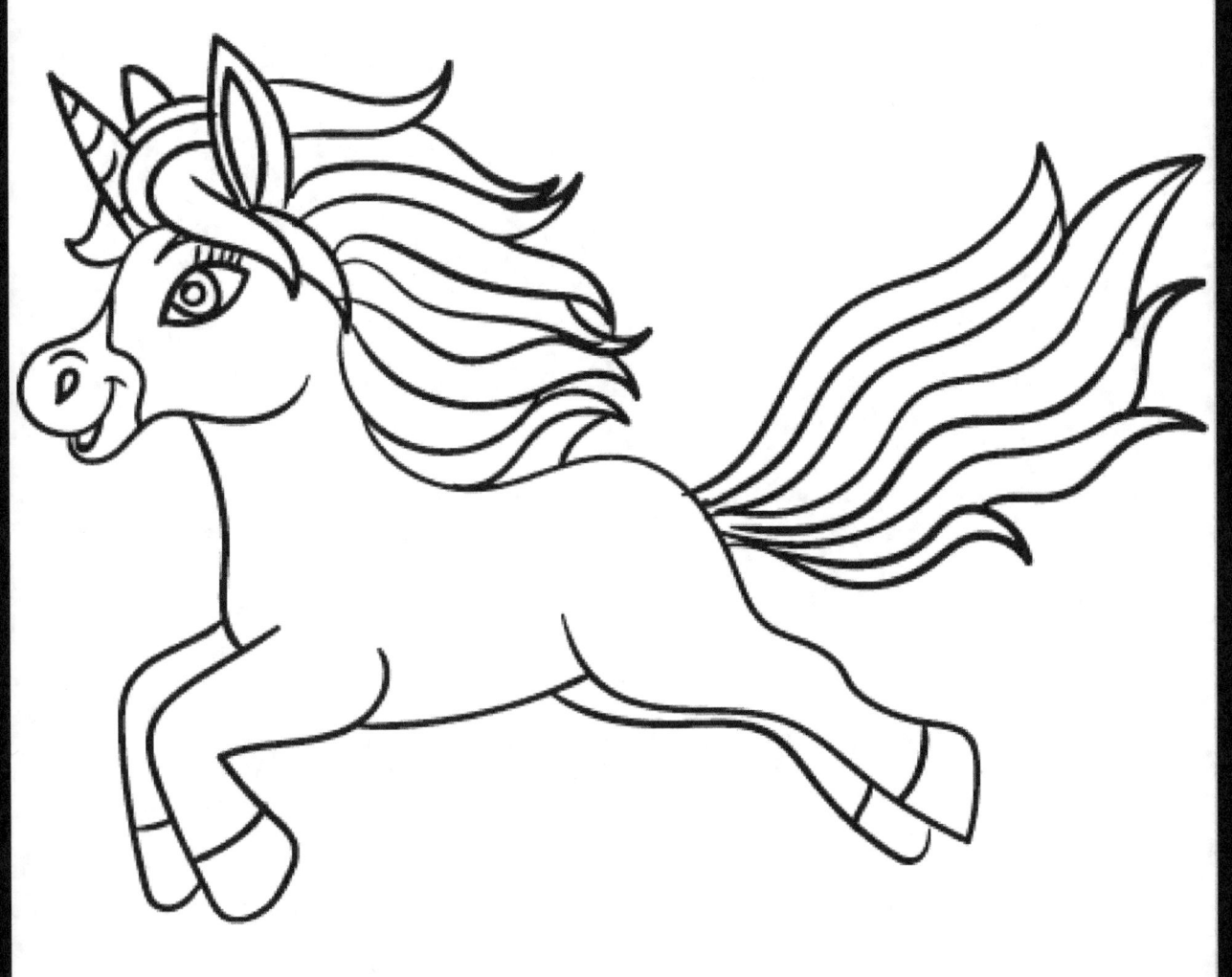

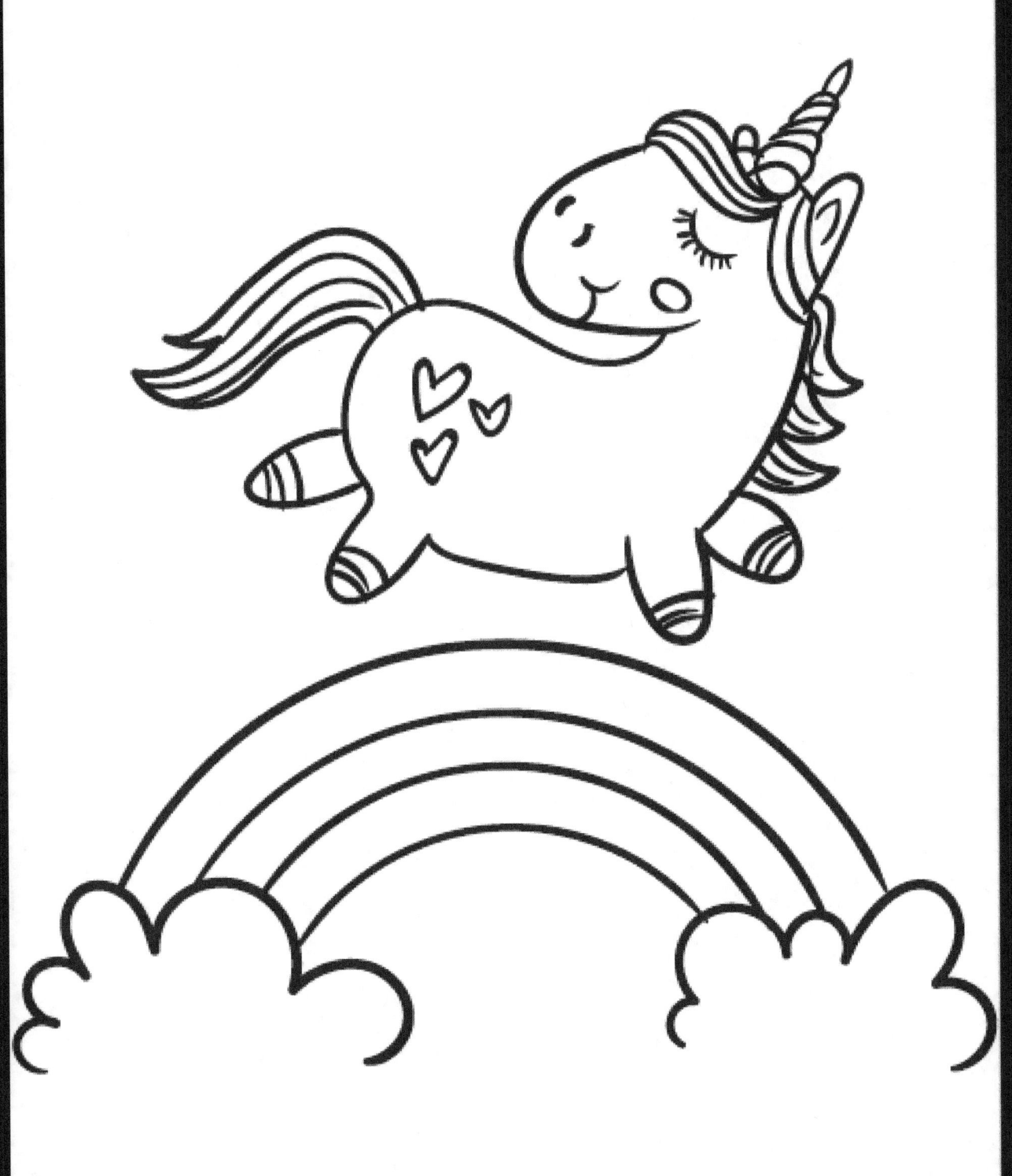

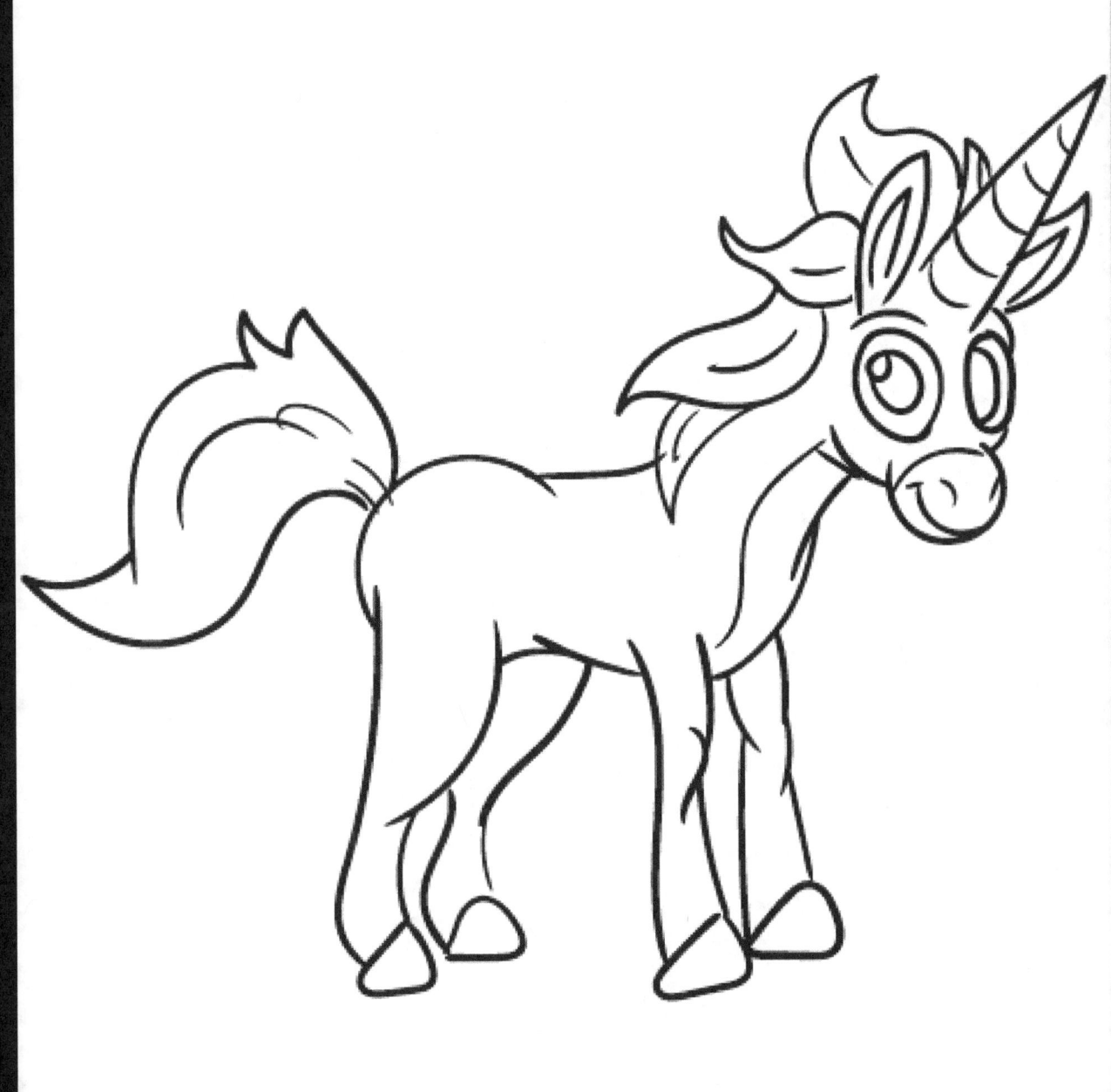

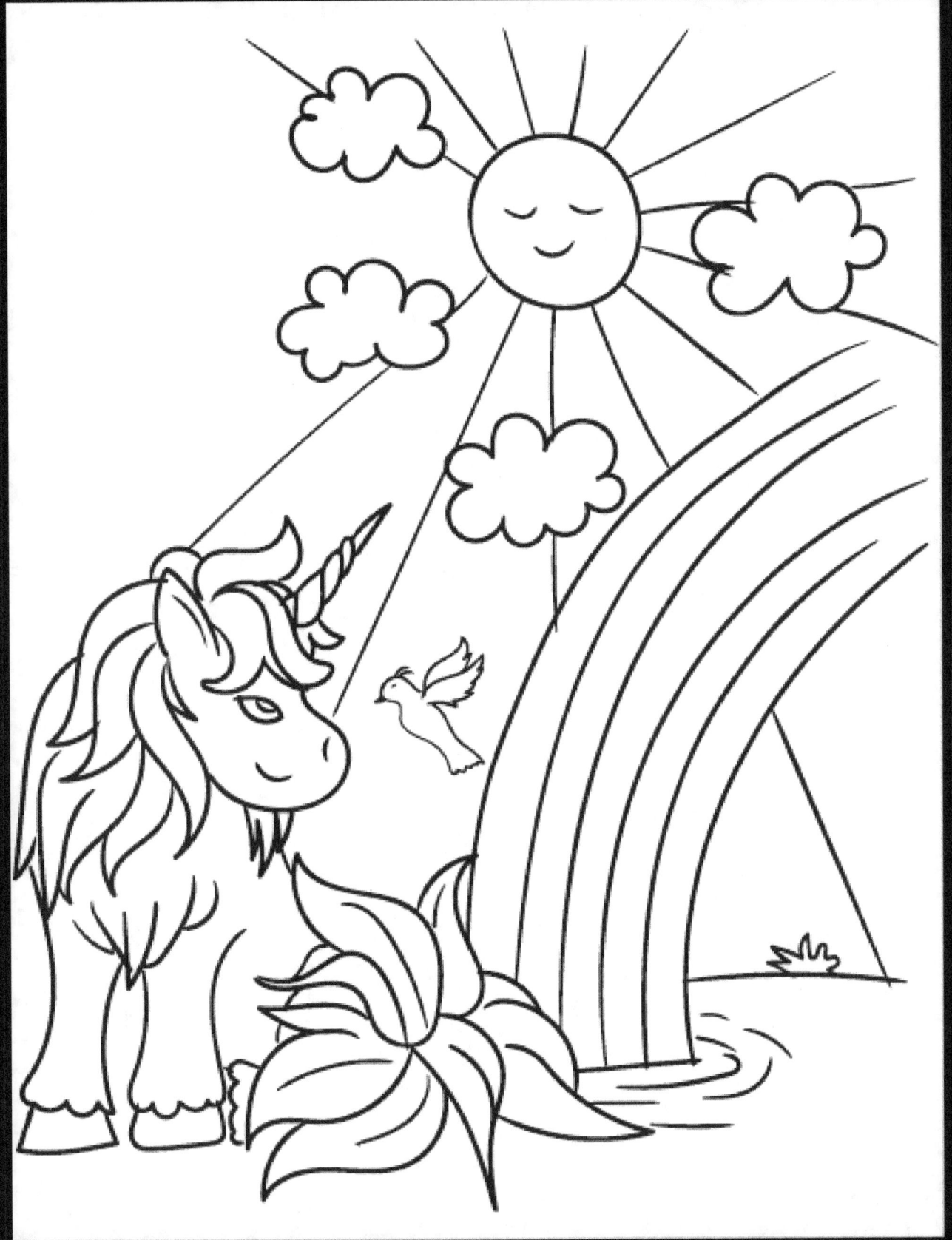

www.ingramcontent.com/pod-product-compliance
Lightning Source LLC
Chambersburg PA
CBHW081102240526
45465CB00026B/3281